DINNER
with
Jane Austen

DINNER *with* Jane Austen

Menus inspired by her novels and letters

PEN VOGLER

CICO BOOKS
LONDON NEW YORK

Published in 2023 by CICO Books

An imprint of Ryland Peters & Small Ltd
20–21 Jockey's Fields
London WC1R 4BW
and 341 East 116th Street
New York NY 10029

www.rylandpeters.com

10 9 8 7 6 5 4 3 2 1

The recipes in this book have been published previously by CICO Books.

A CIP catalog record for this book is available from the Library of Congress and the British Library.

ISBN: 978-1-80065-264-4

Printed in China

Designer: Geoff Borin
Art Director: Sally Powell
Creative Director: Leslie Harrington
Senior Editor: Abi Waters
Editorial Director: Julia Charles
Head of Production: Patricia Harrington
Food Photographer: Stephen Conroy
Home Economist: Emma Jane Frost
Stylist: Luis Peral

NOTES

All recipes serve four unless indicated otherwise.

All eggs are large (UK medium) unless indicated otherwise.

ACKNOWLEDGMENTS

Thanks to Jane Austen's House Museum and to David and Charles for their kind permission to reproduce the version of Martha Lloyd's recipes from *A Jane Austen Household Book*, which have been written out and rationalized by Peggy Hickman; and to Oxford University Press for their kind permission to quote from Jane Austen's letters from their edition by R.W. Chapman.

Renewed thanks to those excellent cooks who generously gave their advice, expertise, and time testing those recipes from *Dinner with Mr. Darcy* that have been reproduced here: Mariateresa Boffo-O'Kane, Isabelle de Cat, Sarah Christie, Ruth Segal, Phoebe Taplin, Jill Vogler, Emma Whiting; and to Jon Vogler for his elegant editorial suggestions. Thanks, too, to the talented team at CICO Books and to Peta Nightingale.

CONTENTS

INTRODUCTION

Were Jane Austen to invite you to dine with her family (setting aside the inconveniences of time travel) what would be unfamiliar?

The dinner hour changed a great deal, even within Jane's lifetime. When her beloved sister Cassandra was staying at stately Godmersham, in 1798, Jane wrote to her from homely Steventon: "We dine now at half after three, & have done dinner I suppose before you begin. – We drink tea at half after six. – I am afraid you will despise us." Jane laughed at this consciousness of social status, but it pushed back the dinner hour for Georgian society. The Netherfield household in *Pride and Prejudice* dined at an achingly fashionable 6.30pm. Mr. Woodhouse, in *Emma*, is old-fashioned enough to enjoy a late supper, serving his guests a delicate, creamy fricassee. After a whirl of dancing, guests at a ball sat down to a candle-lit supper of cold meats, jellies, and spiced wine at around midnight.

Men and women did not walk into the dining room together. Having assembled in the drawing room, the hostess invited the most senior lady present to precede her into the dining room, with all the ladies following in order of rank. In *Persuasion*, the horrible Elizabeth Elliot had, for thirteen years, been "walking immediately after Lady Russell out of all the drawing-rooms and dining-rooms in the country."

On entering the dining room, the dishes were already on the table; a tureen of soup, perhaps roast partridges, and elegantly decorated pies. At Mrs. Bennet's "family dinner" for Mr. Bingley and Mr. Darcy she was determined to impress them with two full courses; after the first course the servants would whip off the top cloth and troop in with more dishes, savory and sweet together.

I hope you enjoy time traveling with these recipes inspired by Jane Austen's slender, but witty and revealing, references to food in her novels and letters.

Mrs. Bennet's Dinner to Impress

PRIDE AND PREJUDICE

Fresh Pea Soup

*

Partridges with Bread Sauce

*

Spiced Mushrooms

*

Everlasting Syllabub

*

Only Jane Austen's most ridiculous characters fuss about food, but it is thanks to the Mrs. Bennets of the novels that we glean so much about what was served and what it all meant. Planning the dinner for fifteen at Longbourn, Mrs. Bennet, anxious that Bingley will marry Jane, decides that nothing less than two full courses would "satisfy the appetite and pride of one who had ten thousand a year." The September menu is suggested here, with some help from her self-congratulatory post-mortem.

"The venison was roasted to a turn—and every body said, they never saw so fat a haunch. The soup was fifty times better than what we had at the Lucas's last week; and even Mr. Darcy acknowledged, that the partridges were remarkably well done; and I suppose he has two or three French cooks at least."

This is an excellent summary of the burning issues for the Georgian hostess: how to better the neighbors; how to stake your claim on the social ladder with game, the food of landowners and aristocracy; and the combination of admiration and suspicion English country folk felt for French food and French chefs.

Mrs. Bennet knows who is worth impressing—not Charlotte Lucas who has to shift with the family: "I hope my dinners are good enough for her." But when Mr. Bennet announces that "a gentleman, and a stranger" is to come to dinner, her first thought is to summon Hill, the cook, and lament that there wouldn't be any fresh fish available to impress her mystery guest.

FRESH PEA SOUP

This recipe comes from the Household Book of Martha Lloyd, a close friend who kept a handwritten collection of recipes from their circle. It gives us a wonderful insight into the dishes that Jane ate with her family and friends, including this Austen family favorite, Pea Soup. Jane wrote that she was not ashamed to invite an unexpected guest to "our elegant entertainment" of "pease-soup, a spare rib and a pudding" (letter to Cassandra, December 1 1798.) This was a perfect way of using up the older peas from the garden to produce a fresh, vividly colored soup.

2 celery sticks, finely chopped

1 onion, finely chopped

Scant ½ stick/50 g butter

Few sprigs of mint and parsley, chopped

3 anchovies or 6–8 anchovy fillets, chopped

Freshly ground white pepper

4 cups/500 g frozen or fresh peas

Generous 1 quart/1 liter light vegetable or chicken stock

Pinch of sugar

4–5 good handfuls of spinach (you could use lettuce and/or chopped cucumber instead of the spinach)

Gently cook the celery and onion in butter until it is soft but not browned, then add the mint, parsley, and anchovy, grind in a little white pepper, and cook for a few minutes.

Stir the peas into the mixture, add the stock and a good pinch of sugar, and simmer for 10 minutes.

Add the spinach (or lettuce and/or cucumber) at the end of the cooking time, and cook for a few minutes more. Let it cool, then whizz with a blender. This gives a nice grainy texture, but push it through a sieve if you would like a smooth soup in the Georgian manner. Reheat gently to serve.

Pease Soup *Take two quarts of pease. Boil them to a pulp. Strain them. Put ½ lb of butter into a stewpan, Celery, half an onion, and stew them til tender. Then put two anchovies, powdered pepper, salt, mint and parsley, (each a small handful) and spinach, and heat of each a small quantity. Half a spoonful of sugar. The soup be boiled as thick as you like it and the whole to be ground together, boiled up and dished.*

MARTHA LLOYD'S HOUSEHOLD BOOK

PARTRIDGES WITH BREAD SAUCE

The partridge recipe is based on William Verral's from *A Complete System of Cookery*, 1759, and the bread sauce recipe comes from *The Cook's Oracle* by William Kitchiner, 1817. The partridges would have been placed before a guest to flatter him as being refined and manly, because shooting game was a noble and masculine pursuit. Mr. Darcy's praise unites him with these qualities in the reader's mind, if not Mrs. Bennet's. Partridge is not hung for long so it has a delicate flavor, which the mild-mannered bread sauce matches well.

4 partridges

Butter

4 partridge livers (or 1 chicken liver quartered)

A few sprigs of parsley or sage leaves, roughly chopped

8 thin rashers streaky unsmoked bacon

Gravy

2 tsp all-purpose (plain) flour

1¼ cups/300 ml hot game or chicken stock

Port wine (optional)

Bread sauce

2 cups/500 ml milk

1 onion, peeled and halved

6 peppercorns or allspice berries and/or a blade of mace

5 slices/150 g two-day-old bread, torn into small pieces (leave it to air-dry slightly if it is fresh)

Pinch of salt

2 tbsp/30 g butter

For the bread sauce, bring the milk to simmering point with the onion, mace, and peppercorns or allspice, and leave it for an hour or two for the spices to flavor the milk.

Remove the onion and flavorings and add the bread to the milk. Leave it for half an hour to swell. Add more bread or milk to get the consistency you want, then throw in the salt and butter.

Preheat the oven to 425°F/220°C/Gas Mark 7.

Rub a little butter on the partridge breasts, put the livers and chopped herbs into the breast cavity, then wrap the bacon around the birds, making sure the breast is covered. Put in a roasting pan.

Roast for 15 minutes, then reduce the heat to 325°F/160°C/Gas Mark 3. Remove the bacon so the partridge breasts can brown, but leave it in the pan to crisp, and roast for another 10 minutes, basting with the pan juices.

Take the partridges and bacon out of the pan, and cover them with foil to rest for a few minutes.

Make the gravy by adding the flour to the juices in the roasting pan over a low heat, beating vigorously with a wooden spoon to remove the lumps. Slowly add the hot game or chicken stock, stirring all the time as it thickens. Add a dash of port if you have some.

Gently heat the bread sauce, mixing well.

To make the traditional liver toast, fry some bread cut into small squares or triangles to make "sippets", and add the mashed livers from the cavity. Serve separately.

SPICED MUSHROOMS

Martha Lloyd has a recipe for drying mushrooms with spices that is adapted here, with the addition of a little wine, for big, fresh field mushrooms. These have an earthy, robust flavor, and would have been in season for Mrs. Bennet's September dinner.

12 small whole shallots, peeled
2 tbsp/30 g butter
1 lb/450 g field mushrooms, quartered
Freshly ground white pepper
¼ tsp ground cloves
½ tsp ground mace
½ tsp grated nutmeg
Sea salt
2–3 bay leaves
Small glass of white or red wine (optional)

Gently cook the shallots in the butter until they are nearly soft – about 15 minutes. Add the mushrooms to the pan with a little more butter if needed, and cook for about 10 minutes until they are brown on all sides and oozing juice. Sprinkle over the spices and salt, add the bay leaves, cover with the wine, if using, and simmer for 10–15 minutes until there is just a little liquid remaining.

If you have a mushroom glut (or want an umami hit) and want to dry them, omit the wine, and leave the mushrooms somewhere very warm, such as the bottom of an Aga, or the top of a woodburner, for a few hours. The dried mushrooms can be powdered and added to stews, or left whole and reconstituted in water.

To Dry Mushrooms *Take a peck of mushrooms without taking out the combs, peel the biggest and wash the others, then put them into a kettle with 12 onions, two handfuls of salt, a good quantity of pepper, cloves, mace, nutmegs and some bay leaves, then hang them on the fire and let them boil till almost all the liquor is consumed, often stirring them about, and when they can boil no longer for fear of burning, stir into them about half a pound of butter, and when they are cold pick them out and lay them singly on earthen platters, and set them into the oven as soon as you have drawn your bread, and so do as often as you like till they are thoroughly dry. Then beat them into a powder, and put it up close in a gallipot; a spoonful of this powder gives a rich taste to any made dish, and helps to thicken the same.*

MARTHA LLOYD'S HOUSEHOLD BOOK

EVERLASTING SYLLABUB

In *Lesley Castle*, the food-obsessed Charlotte Lutterell says "my sister came running to me in the Store-room with her face as White as a Whipt syllabub." Hannah Glasse's version is whipped too, but the earliest versions were made in the dairy by squirting the milk directly from the cow into a bowl of cider or ale.

⅔ cup/150 ml medium sherry or medium sweet white wine

Juice of 1 orange

Zest of 1 lemon

1¼ cups/150 g confectioners' (icing) sugar

2¼ cups/560 ml thick cream

1 tsp natural orange flower water (with no added alcohol)

Put the sherry, orange juice, lemon zest, and confectioners' sugar together in a bowl, and stir well until the sugar dissolves.

In another bowl, beat the cream until it is stiff (Hannah gives it half an hour!), and then fold in the prepared liquid and the orange flower water.

To serve: This could be used as a topping for a jelly, or served simply by itself in pretty wine glasses with a sprig of rosemary or a curl of lemon zest to decorate.

To Make Everlasting Syllabub Take five half pints of thick Cream, and half a Pint of Sack, the Juice of two Seville Oranges, or Lemons, grate in just the yellow Rind of three Lemons, and a Pound of double-refined Sugar well beat, and sifted. Mix all together with a Spoonful of Orange-flower Water, beat it well together with a Whisk half an Hour, then with a Spoon fill your Glasses.

HANNAH GLASSE, *THE ART OF COOKERY MADE PLAIN AND EASY*, 1747

An Autumn Dinner with the Bateses

EMMA

Dried Pea Soup

*

Roast Loin of Pork with Onions

*

Vegetable Pies for Winter and Summer

*

Herb Pie

*

Baked Compote of Apples

*

Old Mrs. Bates and chatty Miss Bates, probably the poorest characters in the major novels, receive, cook, and share food with such gratitude and generosity that their love of eating is remarkably uncensored by their author. They are delighted by the Woodhouses' gift of a hind-quarter of a porker (a young pig raised for pork rather than ham and bacon) and grateful to Mr. Knightley for a sack of apples. They excitedly plan how to "dress" (cook) the pork and share it with a neighbor, and cook the apples to tempt Jane Fairfax's feeble appetite.

They would have a fire over which Patty, their maidservant, makes her excellent apple dumplings and roasts pork. These are hearty dishes for ladies whose warmth in winter must come mostly from their food intake. They could not afford an oven, so bread, cakes, and apples would be sent to Mrs. Wallis, the neighborly baker, who lets them bake apples in her brick oven as it cools overnight.

The Austens, although they had wealthy relatives, had their own domestic cares. At Steventon Rectory they had livestock, including pigs to be slaughtered and preserved. Jane writes that Mrs. Austen, having a pig salted for her seafaring son, "means to pay herself for the salt and the trouble of ordering it to be cured by the sparibs, the souse, and the lard." (Letter to Cassandra, January 21 1799.)

Apples also featured highly in their menus; as Jane wrote to Cassandra, she was pleased to hear a good report of a new cook because, "Good apple pies are a considerable part of our domestic happiness." (Letter, October 17 1815.)

DRIED PEA SOUP

Dried peas had been the stock food of the poor for centuries, either as a thick pease pottage or boiled in a cloth to make pease pudding. It was more genteel to have them in a soup and this would be the perfect way for the Bateses to get the most from the salted leg. I have here adapted an 1806 recipe for 'Old Peas Soup' from Mrs. Rundell's *A New System of Domestic Cookery*.

To boil a ham hock

1 ham hock
1 onion, halved
1 celery stick, roughly chopped
½ tsp black peppercorns
1 bay leaf

If it is salty, soak the ham in water overnight and rinse in a fresh change of water.

Cover it in cold water, add the rest of the ingredients, and bring it to a boil. Simmer on low heat for 2–2½ hours.

When it is cool, sieve the liquid into a measuring cup and make it up to 1 quart/1 liter if you don't have enough (a little over a quart/liter is fine.)

Shred the ham and reserve it for stirring into the soup at the end.

Soup

1 quart/1 liter water from the boiled ham
¾ cup/140 g yellow or green split peas
2 carrots, finely chopped
1 turnip, finely chopped
1 leek, finely chopped
1 celery stick, finely chopped

Add the peas to the ham liquor, bring to a boil, and simmer with a lid on until the peas are mushy, about 50 minutes (or for about 30 minutes if you have soaked them overnight in water).

Add the chopped vegetables, and simmer for another 30 minutes, or until they are cooked through. Add a little more water if it is getting too thick. Let the pea mixture cook a little, then blend it.

Serve with the ham stirred through or on top.

ROAST LOIN OF PORK WITH ONIONS

Mr. Woodhouse hopes the Bateses don't roast their gift "for no stomach can bear roast pork." Minutes later, Miss Bates arrives to gossip about Mr. Elton's marriage, and to thank Mr. Woodhouse because, "My dear sir, if there is one thing my mother loves better than another, it is pork —a roast loin of pork." This recipe is adapted from Hannah Glasse's *The Art of Cookery Made Plain and Easy* from 1747.

3½ lb/1.5 kg loin of pork

Sea salt and freshly ground black pepper

1 tsp vinegar

1–2 tsp olive oil

2¼ lb/1 kg onions

1 tbsp good wine vinegar

2 tsp Dijon mustard or 1 tsp English mustard

Preheat the oven to 425°F/220°C/Gas Mark 7.

Score the skin of the pork, rub it with salt, pepper, and a little vinegar and olive oil, and roast in a large roasting pan in a hot oven for 20 minutes.

Meanwhile, peel and slice the onions into thin rings. After 20 minutes, reduce the heat to 325°F/160°C/Gas Mark 3. Take the pork out of the oven and transfer to a plate, add a little olive oil to the pan and put it back in the oven for 5 minutes to heat. Then add the onion rings, stirring them so they separate into rings and get coated in oil. Put the pork back into the pan and roast for an additional 25 minutes per each pound/450g.

The onions should cook very slowly and become deliciously sweet and sticky. Stir them from time to time, and add a tablespoon of water if they are starting to brown too early, or are looking dry.

When the pork is done, take it out of the oven, cover with foil, and let it rest for 10–15 minutes. Lift the onions into a saucepan, leaving the fat behind in the roasting pan for gravy. Put the saucepan over low heat and let the onions finish cooking for 10 minutes, then add the wine vinegar and mustard, and cook for another 3–4 minutes.

To serve, carve the pork into thick slices, and put the onions in a serving dish to let people help themselves.

VEGETABLE PIES FOR WINTER AND SUMMER

The word "vegetable," as used by Martha Lloyd, was just beginning to replace "garden stuff," "herbs" for leaves, and "pot-herbs" for root vegetables around this time. In the spirit of early cookery books, which often give several different recipes for the same dish (under the heading "another way"), I suggest Martha's veggie pie for winter and Mrs. Rundell's version for summer.

Winter Vegetable Pie

2 parsnips

4 leeks

4 carrots

1 rutabaga (swede)

2 onions

¼ cabbage, about 11 oz/300 g

Butter for frying

Sea salt and freshly ground black pepper or white pepper to taste

1 tsp chopped thyme and/or 2 tsp flat-leaf parsley (optional)

Shortcrust Pastry

1¼ cups/170g all-purpose (plain) flour

Pinch of salt

Scant stick/115g unsalted butter (cold, from the fridge)

2–3 tbsp cold water

Preheat the oven to 375°F/190°C/Gas Mark 5.

First, make the shortcrust pastry. Put the flour and salt into a bowl. Add the cold butter, then chop it with a knife until each piece of butter is as small as you can make it and thoroughly coated in flour. When you can chop no more, rub it in using just your fingertips. Sprinkle in 2 tablespoons of cold water and mix it with a knife until it clumps together. Add a little more water if necessary. Bring it together with your hands to make a smooth dough, but don't knead it. Cover it with plastic wrap (clingfilm) and let it rest in the fridge for 20 minutes before using. Roll it out to an even thickness on a lightly floured surface.

Chop the vegetables and fry them in butter until soft, giving the onions a head start of a few minutes. It should take 20–25 minutes. Add salt and pepper and the herbs if using. Put into a well-buttered pie dish and add a couple tablespoons of water. Cover with shortcrust pastry, make a couple of slashes in the top to let the steam out, and bake for 25–35 minutes. Serve with a good veal, chicken, or onion gravy.

Summer Vegetable Pie

1 cup/100 g shelled fava beans (broad beans) (Start with about 1 lb /450 g beans in their pods)

⅔ cup/100 g fresh peas

4 young carrots

2 baby turnips

2 artichoke bottoms

1½ cups/100 g mushrooms

1 onion

1 crisp lettuce, such as romaine (cos) or Little Gem

4 sticks celery

1 tbsp chopped flat-leaf parsley

Sea salt and freshly ground black pepper or white pepper (optional)

1 batch of shortcrust pastry (see recipe on page 24)

Preheat the oven to 375°F/190°C/Gas Mark 5.

Blanch the fava beans and peas. Cut the other vegetables into cubes and fry in a little butter for 20 minutes until soft. Add the fava beans, peas, and parsley toward the end, and season with a very little salt and pepper, if desired.

Put into a well-buttered pie dish and add a couple of tablespoons of water. Cover with shortcrust pastry, make a couple of slashes in the top to let the steam out, and bake for 25–35 minutes.

Serve with a good veal, chicken, or onion gravy.

Vegetable Pie Take as many vegetables as are in season, cabbage, turnips, carrots, cucumbers and onion. Fry them in butter. When well fry'd drain, and season them with pepper and salt and lay them in layers in your dish. Cover them with a crust, have ready some good gravy to put into the pie when baked. It must not be put into a very hot oven.

MARTHA LLOYD'S HOUSEHOLD BOOK

Vegetable Pie Scald and blanch some broadbeans; cut young carrots, turnips, artichoke bottoms, mushrooms, peas, onions, lettuce, parsley, celery, or any of them you have; make the whole into a nice stew, with some good veal gravy. Bake a crust over a dish, with a little lining round the edge, and a cup turned up to keep it from sinking. When baked, open the lid, and pour in the stew.

MRS. RUNDELL, *A NEW SYSTEM OF DOMESTIC COOKERY*, 1806

HERB PIE

Mrs. Rundell in her book *A New System of Domestic Cookery* from 1806, and her contemporaries, did not distinguish between what we call leaves and herbs. The beauty of her herb pie is that you could use any combination of leaves and add any leafy herbs; even herbs that the Georgians wouldn't recognize, such as cilantro (fresh coriander) or arugula (rocket), would work here.

1¾ lb (about 16 packed cups)/800g of mixed seasonal herbs and greens. Mrs. Rundell uses parsley, spinach, lettuce, mustard, and cress (easy to grow on a windowsill,) borage, and white beet leaves. You could use beet leaves, chard, kale, or spring greens, or add a little mint, dill, or chives.

Sea salt and freshly ground black pepper

Butter, to grease pie dish

2 eggs

1 scant cup/200ml milk

1 generous cup/250ml light (single) cream

2 tbsp all-purpose (plain) flour

1 batch of shortcrust pastry (see recipe on page 24)

Preheat the oven to 375°F/190°C/Gas Mark 5.

Quickly blanch the tougher leaves—spinach, beet, kale, chard stalks—in boiling water, then immediately plunge into cold water. Using your hands, gently squeeze out the excess liquid and chop roughly. Mix with the more delicate leaves, season with salt and pepper, and put aside in a buttered pie dish.

Beat the eggs well, then add the milk and cream, continuing to beat. Thicken with the flour, whisking thoroughly to ensure that there are no lumps, and pour over the mixed greens.

Roll out the shortcrust pastry and cover the pie dish, making a couple of slashes to release moisture. Bake in the oven until the pastry is lightly golden and cooked through, about 30–40 minutes.

BAKED COMPOTE OF APPLES

The Bateses twice-baked apples would be whole, unpeeled apples left over two or three nights in the baker's cooling brick oven until they were, as Eliza Acton says in her recipe for Dried Norfolk Biffins, "the form of small cakes of less than an inch thick." This recipe can be made with a normal domestic oven.

6–8 McIntosh or Cox's orange pippin apples
2 tbsp soft light brown sugar
6–8 small pieces of thin lemon zest

Core the apples. Pack them closely together in a casserole dish, and sprinkle with the sugar and lemon zest. Cover tightly and leave them at 250°F/120°C/Gas Mark ½ or in the bottom of an Aga for 5–7 hours.

To serve: Eliza Acton recommends serving them hot or cold with custard.

Baked Compote of Apples *Put into a wide Nottingham jar, with a cover, two quarts of golden pippins, or of the small apple which resembles them in appearance, called the orange pippin (this is very plentiful in the county of Kent), pared and cored, but without being divided; strew amongst them some small strips of very thin fresh lemon-rind, throw on them, nearly at the top, half a pound of good Lisbon sugar, and set the jar, with the cover tied on, for some hours, or for a night, into a very slow oven. The apples will be extremely good, if not too quickly baked: they should remain entire, but be perfectly tender, and clear in appearance. Add a little lemon-juice when the season is far advanced. These apples may be served hot as a second course dish; or cold, with a boiled custard poured round or over them.*

ELIZA ACTON, *MODERN COOKERY FOR PRIVATE FAMILIES*, 1845

The Ball at Netherfield

PRIDE AND PREJUDICE

White Soup

*

Bath Olivers

*

Salmagundy

*

Flummery

*

A Hedgehog

*

Negus

*

“As for the ball, it is quite a settled thing; and as soon as Nicholls has made white soup enough, I shall send round my cards”, Mr. Bingley tells his sister. White soup was a highlight of ball suppers; we know that there is soup at the ball supper at The Crown Inn in *Emma* because Miss Bates gasps at the range of dishes: “Dear Jane, how shall we ever recollect half the dishes for grandmamma? Soup too! Bless me!” Most of the rest of the food, such as chicken, ham, turkey, cheese, dessert, and fruit, would be served cold, but there would be Negus, a sort of mulled wine, served at the end of the evening, to warm people on their way. Fanny Price goes to bed after the Mansfield ball, “feverish with hope and fears, soup, and negus.”

Suppers were served at midnight or later; the dance before supper was the one for a gentleman to engage his favorite partner, as he would take her into supper and sit beside her. Mrs. Weston’s proposal for a supper of sandwiches for The Crown Inn ball is rejected as “wretched” because it gave no such opportunities for flirting. “A private dance, without sitting down to supper, was pronounced an infamous fraud upon the rights of men and women.”

The table at a private ball would look magnificent with silver, crystal and candles, huge roasts, pyramids of fruit and sweetmeats, and playful dishes in the shape of fruits or animals, or glittering jellies with moons and stars.

WHITE SOUP

This highlight of the Ball Supper was a creamy chicken soup, enriched with veal and almonds. It was found on the most aristocratic tables from Medieval times onward, and earlier versions, known as Queen Soup, or *Potage à la Reine*, or blancmange, were decorated with pomegranate seeds and lemon slices. I have here adapted a 1783 recipe by John Farley from *The London Art of Cookery*.

2 lb/900 g veal bones, chopped

A boiling fowl (with giblets)

6 oz/170 g lean ham

Heaping ⅓ cup/55 g rice

2 anchovy fillets, rinsed of salt

Black peppercorns

Bouquet garni (or a bundle of sweet herbs—as many as possible of thyme, winter savory, parsley, bay leaf, marjoram)

1 large onion, chopped

Half head of celery, chopped (you might also want to add a couple of roughly chopped carrots and leeks to the stock)

2½ quarts/2.35 liters water

To finish

¾ cup/85 g ground almonds

Sea salt

¼–½ cup/60–120 ml cream (or to taste)

Put the veal bones into a large pan and rest the chicken, breast down, on top of them. Add the remaining stock ingredients (including the chicken giblets.)

Add the water and bring to a boil, skimming off the froth and scum. Simmer slowly for 2–3 hours. Take out the chicken and reserve.

When the soup has cooled, strain it through a sieve and let it stand a few hours or overnight. When it is quite cold, skim off the fat from the jelly, return the jelly to a saucepan, and warm it. Add the ground almonds and simmer for 20–30 minutes. Add salt to taste. Cool a little and strain again.

To serve: The original soup would be quite smooth and thin, in which case use the chicken meat for another meal, add the cream and heat to just below boiling. Alternatively, shred some or all of the chicken meat, and return it to the saucepan to heat through with the soup, adding the cream at the last minute. If you wanted a heartier (and less wasteful) version, discard the bones, giblets, and herbs, and blend rather than strain the white mixture.

To Make Ollivers Biscuits *Take 3lb of flour, ½ a pint of small beer barm. Take some milk and warm it a little put it to your barm and lay a spunge, let it lay for one hour. Then take a quarter of a pound of butter and warm up with some milk and mix your spunge and lay it to rise before the fire. Roll it out in thin cakes, bake it in a slow oven. (You must put a little salt in your flour, but not much, use them before the fire before you put them in the oven).*

MARTHA LLOYD'S HOUSEHOLD BOOK

BATH OLIVERS

These savory crackers (biscuits) were devised by William Oliver, an eighteenth-century physician in Bath, after he realized the Bath Buns he had also created were making his fashionable patients even fatter. They are perfect served with the English cheeses that the Georgian "higher sort" were beginning to enjoy.

Makes 30–40 crackers

3¾ cups/500 g all-purpose (plain) flour

¼ oz/7 g sachet active dried yeast

Pinch of salt

2 tbsp/30 g butter

⅔ cup/150 ml milk

Preheat the oven to 325°F/160°C/Gas Mark 3.

Sift the flour into a bowl and add the dried yeast and salt. Warm the butter and milk together, make a well in the flour and slowly add the liquid, stirring the flour into the center until you have a dough. Add some warm water if necessary.

Knead the dough on a floured surface until smooth; put it back in the bowl, cover and let it rise in a warm place for 30 minutes.

Roll out well on a floured surface several times, folding the dough on itself, until it is very thin. Cut out 30–40 crackers with a circular cookie cutter and prick the surface of each one with a fork.

Bake for 20–30 minutes until they are hard and bone-colored; if they are turning color, turn the oven down to 300°F/150°C/Gas Mark 2.

To serve: With a rich local dairy industry, Jane's circle and characters were likely to have often served local cheeses, including the famous Somerset Cheddar. Mr. Elton gives a clue to what a cheese course might consist of when he unromantically describes his whole dinner of the previous night to Harriet, when Emma overtakes them, and finds "that she was herself come in for the Stilton cheese, the north Wiltshire, the butter, the celery, the beet-root and all the dessert." Mrs. Norris happily gets both a receipt for and a sample of "a famous cream cheese" from the housekeeper at Sotherton. Mrs. Austen describes "good Warwickshire cheese" made in the "delightful dairy" at Stoneleigh Abbey.

SALMAGUNDY

This gorgeously presented salad should balance salt, sour, sweet, and savory flavors and offer an invigorating contrast of textures and colors. Hannah Glasse gives three different ways of making and serving it, with the helpful comment that "You may always make a Salamongundy of such things as you have, according to your Fancy". In fact, this salad can be made from almost any ingredients, all chopped small.

Herring

Anchovies (the whole fish, not just the fillets)

Roast chicken, duck, or pigeon meat

Parsley

Cucumber

Apples, peeled (a sprinkling of lemon juice will help keep them from going brown)

Onion, or small pickled onions

Hard-boiled eggs, whites and yolks chopped separately

Pickled gherkins

Celery

Pickled red cabbage

French beans, cooked and sliced

Grapes

Any combination of the following: spinach; sorrel leaves; nasturtium leaves and flowers; watercress

Layer contrasting ingredients on small saucers to form individual, cone-shaped portions, finishing off with a sprig of parsley, or make one big cone and "set an orange or lemon on the top," or put the different ingredients on individual saucers, with the central one raised. Put the saucers on a big plate or clean tray, and decorate around the saucers with watercress, nasturtiums (which Hannah calls "Station Flowers"), cooked French beans, or grapes.

To Make Salamongundy *Take two or three Roman or Cabbage Lettice, and when you have washed them clean, swing them pretty dry in a Cloth; then beginning at the open End, cut them cross-ways, as fine as a good big Thread, and lay the Lettices so cut, about an Inch thick all over the Bottom of a Dish, take a Couple of cold roasted Pullets, or Chickens, and cut the Flesh off the Breasts and Wings into Slices, about three Inches long, a Quarter of an Inch broad, and as thin as a Shilling; lay them upon the Lettice round the End to the Middle of*

the dish, and the other towards the Brim; then having boned and cut six Anchovies, each into eight Pieces, lay them all between each Slice of the Fowls, then cut the lean Meat off the Legs into Dice, and cut a Lemon into small Dice; then mince the Yolk of four Eggs, three or four Anchovies, and little Parsley, and make a round Heap of these in your Dish, piling it up in the Form of a Sugar-loaf, and garnish it with Onions, as big as the Yolk of Eggs, boiled in a good deal of Water very tender and white. Put the largest of the Onions in the Middle on the Top of the Salamongundy, and lay the rest all round the Brim of the Dish, as thick as you can lay them; then beat some Sallat-Oil up with Vinegar, Salt and Pepper, and pour over it all. Garnish with Grapes just scalded, or French Beans blanched, or Station Flowers, and serve it up for a first Course.

HANNAH GLASSE, *THE ART OF COOKERY MADE PLAIN AND EASY*, 1747

FLUMMERY

Flummery is a white jelly, which was set in elegant molds or as shapes within a clear jelly. Its delicate, creamy taste goes particularly well with rhubarb, strawberries, and raspberries. My adaptation is based on a recipe in *The Experienced English Housekeeper* by Elizabeth Raffald from 1769. A modern version would be to add puréed fruit to the ingredients, omitting the same volume of fluid.

5 gelatin leaves

1¼ cups/300 ml milk

½ cup/50 g ground almonds

1–2 tbsp superfine (caster) sugar

1 tsp natural rosewater (with no added alcohol)

A drop of natural almond extract

1¼ cups/300 ml heavy (double) cream

Put the gelatin in a bowl and cover with cold water; leave for 4–5 minutes.

Pour the milk, almonds, and sugar into a saucepan and heat slowly until just below boiling.

Squeeze out the excess water from the gelatin leaves and add them to the almond milk, along with the rosewater, and the almond extract. Simmer for a few minutes, keeping it below boiling point. Let it cool a little and strain it through cheesecloth, or a very fine sieve.

Whip the cream until thick, and then fold it into the tepid mixture. Wet your molds (essential, to make it turn out), put in the flummery and leave to stand in the fridge overnight.

To serve: If you don't have a jelly mold with a removable lid, dip the mold briefly into boiling water before turning out the flummery.

A HEDGEHOG

This delicate marzipan is made into a hedgehog with almonds for the spines and dried currants for eyes. Although we might make it for a child's birthday, it would have been made to amuse adult guests, served on a pool of flavored cream or jelly.

2½ cups/250 g ground almonds

¾–1 cup/120–140 g confectioner's (icing) sugar

A little natural orange flower or rosewater (with no added alcohol) or orange juice

Half almonds or slivered (flaked) almonds

Currants for the eyes (and nose, if you like)

Preheat the oven to 350°F/180°C/Gas Mark 4.

Mix the ground almonds and sugar well together; add the liquid, a teaspoonful at a time, until you have a thick, moldable paste that doesn't crack (like marzipan).

Hannah makes this paste into one big hedgehog, using almonds for the spines, and currants for the eyes. I think it is nicer to make it into little ones (or one bigger one and a few little ones,) and bake them for 10 minutes or so until the outsides are golden brown. This is the sweetmeat called "marchpane" in Tudor times; it has a lovely, chewy texture and is nicer than raw marzipan.

To make a hedgehog *Take two Quarts of sweet blanched Almonds, beat them well in a Mortar, with a little Canary and Orange-flower Water, to keep them from oiling. Make them into a stiff Paste, then beat in Sugar, put in half a Pound of sweet Butter melted, set on a Furnace, or slow Fire, and keep it constantly stirring till it is stiff enough to be made into the Form of a Hedge-Hog, then put it into a Dish.*

HANNAH GLASSE, *THE ART OF COOKERY MADE PLAIN AND EASY*, 1747

NEGUS

This mulled wine, created by Colonel Francis Negus (d.1732) was served at the balls in *Mansfield Park* and *The Watsons*, and was often offered to guests before their chilly journey home. By Victorian times it was thought to be the thing for children's birthday parties! This version, which is safer served to adults, is based on an original from Mrs. Beeton's *Book of Household Management* (1861).

Serves 16–20

1 x 25 fl oz/75 cl bottle of port

3 cups/750 ml water

1–2 tbsp brown sugar

Zest and juice of 1 lemon

About 1 tsp freshly grated nutmeg

1 cinnamon stick and/or 8 whole cloves (optional)

Segments of orange and/or lemon, to serve

Put the water in a saucepan and add the lemon zest, a tablespoon of sugar and the spices. Bring it to a boil and let it simmer very gently for 10–15 minutes. Add the lemon juice.

Strain, return to the saucepan, and reheat. Pour in the port; taste it, and add a little more sugar if you like. Heat very gently to serving temperature. Put slices of lemon and/or orange into glasses before pouring in the Negus, or serve it from a pitcher (jug).

An Old-fashioned Supper for Mr. Woodhouse and his Guests

EMMA

Toasted Cheese

*

Fricassee of Sweetbreads with Asparagus

*

Buttered Apple Tart

*

Poor Knights

*

In Jane's early years, when dinner was usually taken in mid-afternoon, supper might be quite a substantial meal, served at nine or ten o'clock at night. By the time she wrote *Emma* (published in 1814–15), the fashionable dinner hour was so much later that a hot supper was outdated; Mr. Woodhouse "loved to have the cloth laid, because it had been the fashion of his youth."

Supper would be taken in the drawing room (or the supper room if the house is, like Northanger Abbey, large enough to have one) and eaten from small tables. It was served after the evening's entertainment, perhaps the theatre, if in town, or music or card games at home. The Bennet girls' aunt Philips invites them to join her party after dinner for a vulgar, but fun "nice comfortable noisy game of lottery tickets, and a little bit of hot supper afterwards."

Mr. Woodhouse enjoys inviting his elderly neighbors for a proper old-fashioned supper of "made" dishes, such as sweetbreads with asparagus, scalloped oysters, and minced chicken, and recommending foods that he considers "not unwholesome." He would surely have disapproved of the supper the Austens provided for guests in Southampton—a tray of wigeon and preserved ginger ("as delicious as one could wish") and black butter (a sort of apple preserve), which was "not at all what it ought to be; it was neither solid nor entirely sweet." (Letter to Cassandra, December 27 1808.) Supper, often whatever one fancied, and eaten with intimate friends, was a cozy meal, such as the one Jane describes having with the family's benefactress, Mrs. Knight, when they shared tart and jelly in her dressing room.

TOASTED CHEESE

When Fanny Price stays with her parents, she finds the house a maelstrom of people; her father calling for rum and water, her little brothers begging for toasted cheese for supper. Jane remarks to Cassandra on the hospitality of a gentleman who "made a point of ordering toasted cheese for supper entirely on my account." (Letter, August 27 1805.)

4 whole salted anchovies or 8–12 anchovy fillets

4 slices sourdough or Italian bread, such as ciabatta

A little olive oil

Garlic clove (optional)

7oz/200 g Parmesan cheese or other strong cheese, such as mature Cheddar, grated

Put a baking tray in the oven and preheat to 400°F/200°C/Gas Mark 6.

Rinse the anchovies and pat them dry with paper towel. Drizzle a little olive oil on the breads and, if you like, rub them with the cut side of a garlic clove.

Cut the whole anchovies longways into two and lay them or the fillets on the bread. Put them on the hot baking tray, cover with the grated cheese, and bake for about 10–12 minutes until the cheese is melted and the edges are browned.

Alternatively, toast one side of the bread, lay the anchovies and cheese (with oil and optional garlic) on the untoasted side as before, and let it brown under the broiler (grill) for 5–6 minutes.

Anchovies, with Parmesan Cheese *Fry some bits of bread about the length of an anchovy in good oil or butter, lay the half of an anchovy, with the bone upon each bit, and strew over them some Parmesan cheese grated fine, and colour them nicely in an oven, or with a salamander*, squeeze the juice of an orange or lemon, and pile them up in your dish and send them to table. This seems to be but a trifling thing, but I never saw it come whole from table.*

WILLIAM VERRAL, A COMPLETE SYSTEM OF COOKERY, 1759

** A salamander was an iron disc with a wooden handle, heated in the coals until it glowed red, and then held over dishes to grill them.*

FRICASSEE OF SWEETBREADS WITH ASPARAGUS

Mrs. Bates is disappointed when that old fusspot Mr. Woodhouse fancies the asparagus undercooked, and sends it back. Perhaps his cook, Searle, had been reading William Verral's *A Complete System of Cookery* (1759), as he recommends boiling the asparagus for this dish, "not so much as we boil them to eat with butter".

4 lamb sweetbreads (the stomach sweetbreads are the best ones to use; they are bigger and rounder than the thymus ones, which have a tendency to fall apart)

Flour, seasoned with salt, pepper, nutmeg

1½ cups/100 g white button mushrooms, finely chopped

1 scallion (spring onion), chopped

Knob of butter

Bundle of asparagus (about 18 spears)

Small glass of white wine

1 tbsp parsley, finely chopped

Sea salt and freshly ground black pepper to taste

Squeeze of lemon juice to taste

To prepare the sweetbreads, soak them for 2–3 hours in cold water, changing the water 3 or more times until they are white.

Put them in a pan of fresh water, bring it to a boil and simmer for 3–4 minutes. Take them out and put them into iced water. Once they are thoroughly cooled, trim away any visible gristle and large veins from the exterior (easiest done using your fingers.) Do not try and remove all of the finer membranes, or the sweetbreads will fall apart completely.

Dry them thoroughly, then slice them, coat them in the seasoned flour, and fry until each side is golden and lightly crisped. Remove from the pan and keep warm. To the same (uncleaned) pan, add the mushrooms and scallion and a knob of butter, and cook over medium heat for a few minutes.

Meanwhile steam or boil the asparagus lightly. Add the white wine to the mushroom pan, let it boil, and reduce for a minute or two, then add the parsley, and salt and pepper to taste. Return the sweetbreads to the pan briefly, then serve the mixture with the asparagus on top and a squeeze of lemon.

BUTTERED APPLE TART

Mr. Woodhouse reassures Miss Bates that he is offering her a tart made from fresh apples and "You need not be afraid of unwholesome preserves here. I do not advise the custard." I hope you disregard Mr. Woodhouse's views on custard and enjoy this unusual but happy marriage of egg custard and apple tart based on the recipe from Hannah Glasse's book *The Art of Cookery Made Plain and Easy* (1747).

- 4–5 cooking apples
- 2 tbsp/30 g butter
- 2–4 tbsp sugar
- ½ tsp grated nutmeg
- ½ tsp ground cinnamon (optional — not in original recipe)
- Juice and zest of 1 orange
- 1 pack of store-bought sweet shortcrust pastry
- 3 eggs, separated
- Confectioners' (icing) sugar, to serve

Skin, core, and slice the apples and cook them in a tablespoon of water until just soft. While the apples are hot, stir in the butter, sugar to taste, the nutmeg, and cinnamon if using, and the orange zest and juice.

While the mixture cools, preheat the oven to 375°F/190°C/Gas Mark 5, and line a 10-inch/25cm pie dish with the pastry.

Beat the egg yolks and stir them into the apple. Whisk the egg whites to stiff peaks and fold them into the mixture. Pour the mixture into the pastry case and bake for approximately 30 minutes until the eggs are set.

Serve with a dusting of confectioners' sugar over it.

To Make Poor Knights Cut a couple of Penny Loaves into round Slices, and dip them in half a Pint of Cream or Water; then lay then spred in a Dish, and beat up three Eggs with Cream, Sugar and Nutmeg grated. Then melt Butter in a Frying-pan; wet the Sides of the Toasts, and lay them in the Frying-pan the wet Sides downwards, then pour the rest of the Cream, Eggs etc upon them and fry them; when they are done, serve them up with Butter, Sugar and Rose-water.

JOHN NOTT, *THE COOK'S AND CONFECTIONER'S DICTIONARY*, 1723

POOR KNIGHTS

This, or "Poor Knights of Windsor"—perfect for Sir Walter Elliot of Kellynch Hall—is the old name for the supper dish that Hannah Glasse calls "pain perdu" or "cream toasts" and which we know as French Toast or Eggy Bread. The toasts were also sometimes made with wine; a drop of rum or brandy makes them a fine dish for the end of the evening.

4 eggs
1 scant cup/200 ml milk
2 tsp rum or brandy (optional)
A little grated nutmeg
½ cup/100 g caster sugar
8 slices soft day-old bread or brioche, crusts removed and cut in half diagonally
1 stick/125 g unsalted butter

Preheat the oven to 225°F/110°C/Gas Mark ¼.

Combine the eggs, milk, and nutmeg (and rum or brandy if using), and beat in the sugar until it is dissolved.

Pour the mixture into a flat dish so that you can lay the slices of bread flat. Let them soak up the mixture for a few minutes on each side.

Heat the butter in a frying pan until it is foaming, and fry the bread for a couple of minutes on each side until golden. You will need to do them in batches, wiping out the pan after each, and keeping them warm in the oven while you finish the remainder.

To serve: John Nott serves them with a mix of butter, sugar, and rosewater, warmed together and poured over the toasts. They are very good with sharp stewed fruit, such as rhubarb or berries.

Christmas with the Musgroves and other Celebrations

PERSUASION

Roast Leg of Mutton Stuffed with Oysters

*

Braised Turkey

*

Plum Cake

*

Mince Pies

*

The old-fashioned warmth and hospitality of the elder Musgroves is a foil to the chilly self-consciousness of Bath society, never more so than at Christmas, one of the only times that food is mentioned in *Persuasion*. When Anne Elliot and Lady Russell call on the Musgroves in the Christmas holidays, they find a "fine family-piece" of chattering girls and riotous boys, with "tressels and trays, bending under the weight of brawn and cold pies."

Christmas pies could be huge affairs—Hannah Glasse's Yorkshire Christmas Pie has a pigeon, partridge, fowl, goose, and turkey boned and stuffed inside each other—or they might be mince pies, much loved since medieval times. Brawn, made from the face meats of a pig, set in jelly, is (to us) a strange special treat, but made when the pigs were slaughtered in November, it went with the time of year.

Roast beef was England's top celebratory dish, but turkeys had become popular since their introduction from America in the sixteenth century. Jane writes to Martha Lloyd about the "pleasant duties" at Christmas of giving to the poor and "eating Turkies" (November 29 1812.) Geese were fattened up throughout harvest time, and eaten at Michaelmas (September 29); Jane has a Michaelmas goose at Godmersham in 1813, and Harriet is entrusted with one as a seasonal gift in *Emma*.

Plum (meaning dried fruit) puddings would have been eaten throughout the season, but it took Dickens to make them synonymous with Christmas pudding. Lavish fruit cakes were eaten at Twelfth Night, rather than Christmas, in Georgian times, and also, as we know from the one that so alarms Mr. Woodhouse, at weddings.

ROAST LEG OF MUTTON STUFFED WITH OYSTERS

On Christmas Eve, Emma meets Mr. John Knightley with his boys on their way home to eat roast mutton and rice pudding; that evening a saddle of mutton was served at the Westons' dinner party. Oysters and anchovies were often used to intensify the flavor of the mutton, which was the most commonly eaten meat in Georgian times. I have here adapted a recipe from Hannah Glasse's *The Art of Cookery Made Plain and Easy* (1747).

Serves 6–8

A leg of mutton, part boned, 5½–6¾ lb/2.5–3kg (mutton is stronger and less fatty than lamb and is ideal for this dish, but if you cannot source it, use lamb, or hogget which is a sheep of between 1 and 2 years old)

For the stuffing

1 cup/50 g fresh white breadcrumbs

3½ tbsp/50 g suet

2–3 whole salted anchovies (or 8–12 fillets), well rinsed

3 hard-boiled egg yolks

1 shallot, finely chopped

1–2 tsp chopped thyme

1–2 tsp chopped winter savory

12 oysters (keep the liquor for the sauce)

¼ tsp grated nutmeg

1 egg, beaten

For the gravy

Oyster liquor

A wine glass of good dry red wine

1 salted anchovy, or 3–4 anchovy fillets, finely chopped

A little nutmeg

1 small onion

A few oysters (but not essential)

Preheat the oven to 425°F/220°C/Gas Mark 7.

Chop, but do not mash, all the ingredients for the stuffing very finely, except the oysters, which should be left whole. Bind with the raw egg. The leg of mutton should have the shank bone in, and a cavity at the top for your stuffing; push it down as far as it will go, fold the top flaps over the stuffing and tie it tightly with kitchen string.

Hannah advises roasting the meat and boiling the sauce separately, but I part-roast the meat in a preheated oven for 30 minutes, turn the oven down to 325°F/160°C/Gas Mark 3 and pour the ingredients for the gravy around the mutton. Roast for 15–20 minutes per lb/450g.

When the meat is done, put it on a separate plate, cover with foil and let it rest for 15–20 minutes while you skim the fat off the gravy.

BRAISED TURKEY

Turkey was enjoyed all year round, as well as at Christmas—but only by the wealthy. As Mary Crawford says: "A large income is the best recipe for happiness I ever heard of. It certainly may secure all the myrtle and turkey part of it." This is an excellent way of keeping a turkey moist during cooking and is based on William Verral's recipe in *A Complete System of Cookery* (1759).

Serves 6–8

One turkey, 9 lb/4 kg (this will also work for chicken)

6–8 rashers streaky bacon (in squares, plus a larding needle; or strips)

White pepper

1 tsp spices (such as mustard powder, ground nutmeg, cayenne pepper, or ground allspice)

Parsley, finely chopped

For the braise

4 small onions, roughly chopped

6 carrots, roughly chopped

1 turnip, roughly chopped

Head of celery, washed and chopped

Bouquet garni or any of bay leaves, thyme, marjoram, parsley

½ lb/225 g chestnuts

Turkey giblets (optional)

1 quart/liter light stock (chicken or vegetable)

For the salpicon

A salpicon is simply a mix of ingredients chopped small, sometimes bound with a liquid.

1 veal sweetbread (or liver), chopped small (See sweetbread recipe on page 49 for instructions for preparing sweetbreads)

3 mushrooms, diced

2 slices ham, cut small

2 gherkins, diced

A little gravy

Small glass of white wine

Beurre manié (butter and flour, blended in equal quantities)

Sea salt and white pepper

A little chopped parsley

Squeeze of lemon juice

Preheat the oven to 325°F/160°C/Gas Mark 3.

Try to get hold of a larding needle, which will allow you to sew the bacon onto the turkey. If not, use strips of bacon draped over the breast. Season your bacon squares with pepper, any of the spices you fancy, and parsley.

Put the turkey in a big pot or heavy-based roasting pan, surrounded by the vegetables, herbs, chestnuts, and giblets, if using, and cover the vegetables with light stock. Cook in the oven for 20 minutes per lb/450g, basting it now and again. It is ready when the juices run clear when you insert a metal skewer into the meat. Take it out of the oven and let it rest out of the braising liquor for 20 minutes while you finish off the gravy.

Take the chestnuts out of the braise, to be served around the turkey; sieve the liquid, pushing some of the vegetables through the sieve to help thicken it, then reduce it in a saucepan over high heat. Serve this gravy separately.

For the salpicon, sauté the sweetbread or liver and the mushrooms in a little butter or oil, add the ham, gherkins, a little gravy (or stock taken from the turkey as it cooks,) and the white wine. Let it simmer for 5–10 minutes, and if necessary, thicken with the beurre manié and cook for a few minutes longer. Check for seasoning and add the parsley and a squeeze of lemon juice.

To serve: William Verral pours his salpicon over the turkey, but I imagine it would get rather lost, so suggest serving it up separately.

PLUM CAKE

My version of plum cake is based on a recipe from Mrs. Rundell's *A New System of Domestic Cookery* (1806). "Plum" means dried fruit, and rich plum cakes were made for Twelfth Night revels and weddings. Mr. Woodhouse tries to persuade Mr. Perry, the apothecary, that they are indigestible. "There was a strange rumour in Highbury of all the little Perrys being seen with a slice of Mrs. Weston's wedding-cake in their hands: but Mr. Woodhouse would never believe it."

1¼ cups/170 g currants
1¼ cups/170 g raisins
2 tbsp/30 ml brandy
2 tbsp/30 ml sweet wine
1¾ cups/225 g self-rising flour
¾ tsp ground mace
¾ tsp grated nutmeg
½ tsp ground cloves
½ tsp ground allspice
2 sticks/225 g butter
1 heaping cup/225 g soft dark brown sugar
Grated zest of ½ lemon
4 eggs, beaten
Heaping ½ cup/60 g ground almonds
¾ cup/60 g slivered (flaked) almonds
¼ cup/60 ml cream or milk

Leave the dried fruit to soak in the brandy and wine overnight.

Preheat the oven to 300°F/150°C/Gas Mark 2.

Sift the flour and spices together.

Cream the butter with the sugar and lemon zest until pale and fluffy. Beat in the eggs, a little at a time; if the mixture starts to curdle, throw in a little flour to stabilize it.

Fold in the remaining flour and then stir in the rest of the ingredients.

Butter a deep 8-inch/20cm cake pan with a removable base, and line it with 2 thicknesses of parchment paper. Line the outside with two thicknesses of foil or brown paper, tied with string.

Spoon the mixture into the pan and bake for 3 hours, or until a toothpick inserted into the center comes out clean. If it starts to brown too early, cover with layers of foil or parchment paper.

MINCE PIES

Mince pies were originally made with mutton, beef, or tongue, but this was becoming optional by the eighteenth century. "If you chuse Meat in your Pies, parboil a Neat's-Tongue, peel it, and chop the Meat as fine as possible, and mix with the rest," writes Hannah Glasse. Hers is quite a boozy mincemeat; delicious! She suggests making several small pies, as we do, or one slightly larger one.

For the mincemeat

Scant ½ cup/100 g suet, shredded

7 oz/200 g apples, cored and chopped

1 heaping cup/150 g raisins

Heaping 1½ cups/160 g currants

¼ cup/50 g brown sugar

1 tsp ground mace

¼ tsp ground cloves

½ tsp nutmeg

3 tbsp/45 ml brandy

3 tbsp/45 ml sherry

For the pie

Double batch of shortcrust pastry (see recipe on page 24)

A neat's tongue (a beef [ox] tongue) or about 1¼ cups/200 g boiled beef or tongue, chopped small (optional)

Scant ½ cup/50 g candied peel

Zest of 1 orange

Juice of ½ lemon or ½ orange

2 tbsp/30 ml red wine

Make the mincemeat by mixing together the suet, apples, dried fruit, sugar, spices, brandy, and sherry.

Preheat the oven to 400°F/200°C/Gas Mark 6.

Line a pie dish with shortcrust pastry, then add the following: a thin layer of meat (such as beef or tongue, chopped small); a thin layer of citron (candied peel will do); a good layer of mincemeat; a layer of thinly cut orange zest; finishing with a thin layer of meat.

Mix together the juice of half a lemon or half an orange with 2 tablespoons of red wine and sprinkle this over, before covering with a pastry lid.

Bake for 25–35 minutes.

ation: Lemon mincemeat, a pleasant, light version, was popular for Christmas pies. It was made with the addition of a lemon boiled and mashed to a pulp. Martha Lloyd has a recipe for it, and so does Duncan MacDonald, the cook at the Bedford Tavern in London's Covent Garden and author of *The New London Family Cook*. Jane knew of the tavern; in *Northanger Abbey*, John Thorpe tries to impress Catherine by saying he knows General Tilney because "I have met him forever at the Bedford."

Lemon Mincemeat *Squeeze a lemon, boil the outside til tender enough to beat to a mash, add to it three apples chopped, four ounces of suet, half a pound of currants, four ounces of sugar, put the juice of a lemon and candied fruit as for other pies. Make a short-crust and fill the patty pans.*

DUNCAN MACDONALD, *THE NEW LONDON FAMILY COOK*, 1808

To make Mince-Pies the best way *Take three Pounds of Suet shread very fine, and chopped as small as possible, two Pounds of raisings stoned, and chopped as fine as possible, two Pounds of Currans, nicely picked, washed, rubbed, and dried at the Fire, half a hundred of fine Pippins, pared, cored, and chopped small, half a Pound of fine Sugar pounded fine, a quarter of an Ounce of Mace, a quarter of an Ounce of Cloves, two large Nutmegs, all beat fine; put all together into a great Pan, and mix it well together with half a Pint of Brandy, and half a Pint of Sach; put it down close in a Stone-pot, and it will keep good four Months. When you make your Pies, take a little Dish, something bigger than a Soop-plate, lay a very thin Crust all over it, lay a thin Layer of Meat, AND THEN A THIN Layer of Citron cut very thin, then a Layer of Mince meat, and a thin Layer of Orange-peel cut thin, over that a little Meat; squeeze half the Juice of a fine Sevile Orange, or Lemon, and pour in three Spoonfuls of Red Wine; lay on your Crust, and bake it nicely.*

HANNAH GLASSE, *THE ART OF COOKERY MADE PLAIN AND EASY*, 1747

INDEX

BIBLIOGRAPHY

Eliza Acton, *Modern Cookery for Private Families*, 1845
Isabella Beeton, *The Book of Household Management*, 1861
John Farley, *The London Art of Cookery*, 1783
Hannah Glasse, *The Art of Cookery Made Plain and Easy*, 1747
William Kitchiner, *The Cook's Oracle*, 1817
Martha Lloyd's Household Book
Duncan MacDonald, *The New London Family Cook*, 1808
John Nott, *The Cook's and Confectioner's Dictionary*, 1723
Elizabeth Raffald, *The Experienced English Housekeeper*, 1769
Mrs. Rundell, *A New System of Domestic Cookery*, 1806
William Verral, *A Complete System of Cookery*, 1759